JUNIOR SURVIVAL LIBRARY

Jaws in the Water

THE CROCODILE
AND
THE ALLIGATOR

Malcolm Penny

Irwin Publishing
Toronto, Canada

Key to abbreviations

gm	**gram**
kg	**kilogram**
cm	**centimetre**
m	**metre**
km	**kilometre**
km²	**square kilometre**
km/h	**kilometres per hour**

Copyright © 1991 by Irwin Publishing
First published in 1990 by Boxtree Limited,
London, England
Copyright © 1990 Survival Anglia Limited
Text copyright © 1990 Malcolm Penny

Front jacket photograph:
Survival Anglia/Dieter and Mary Plage
(Marsh mugger crocodile; Wilpath National Park,
Sri Lanka)
Back jacket photograph:
Survival Anglia/Jeff Foot
(American alligators)

Line drawings by Raymond Turvey

Edited by Miranda Smith
Designed by Groom & Pickerill
Typeset by Rowland Phototypesetting Limited
Bury St Edmunds, Suffolk

Printed and bound in Italy
by OFSA s.p.a.

for Irwin Publishing,
1800 Steeles Avenue West
Concord, Ontario,
Canada
L4K 2P3

Canadian Cataloguing in Publication Data
Penny, Malcolm
    Jaws in the water : the crocodile and the alligator.

(Junior survival library)
Includes index.
ISBN 0-7725-1837-8 (bound)   ISBN 0-7725-1842-4 (pbk.)

1. Crocodiles – Juvenile literature.   2. Alligators
– Juvenile literature.   I. Title.   II. Title:
The crocodile and the alligator.   III. Series: Junior
survival library (Toronto, Ont.).

QL666.C925P45 1991   j597.98   C91-093178-X

Contents

The largest living reptiles

Reptiles are **cold-blooded**, air-breathing animals, which usually reproduce by laying eggs. Snakes, lizards and turtles are all reptiles, and so were the dinosaurs. But the largest living reptiles are the crocodilians, the group which contains crocodiles and alligators.

They are often called 'primitive' animals, because **fossil** crocodilians which died 65 million years ago look almost exactly the same as those living today. In fact, they are more advanced than other reptiles. A crocodilian's blood system is more efficient at carrying oxygen, so its brain is better developed. This in turn means that it is more intelligent, and able to learn from experience.

Crocodilians are well adapted for life in water. Their eyes, ears and nostrils are set high on their head, so that they can still see, hear and breathe when they are almost completely submerged. When they dive, their nostrils and ears close, to keep the water out, and a transparent inner eyelid closes to protect their eyes.

A Nile crocodile soaks up the heat of the sun with the bright yellow lining of its mouth.

An American alligator, at home in the swamps of the Florida Everglades.

Although reptiles are called 'cold-blooded', compared with 'warm-blooded' birds and mammals, this is not a very good description. What it really means is that reptiles cannot control their body temperature from within. Instead, they control it by their behaviour, moving into the sun to **bask** when they are too cold, and into the shade when they are too hot. Crocodilians spend a large part of each day basking on land, to warm up after they have been swimming.

The only difference between a crocodile and an alligator is in their teeth: an alligator's large fourth lower teeth fit into sockets in its upper jaw, so that they are invisible when the alligator's mouth is shut. A crocodile's fourth teeth are clearly visible. Apart from this small difference, their lives and behaviour are very similar.

Although crocodiles and alligators are very similar, they are able to live in a wide variety of places, and on many different diets. Later, we shall consider why most people fear and dislike crocodilians more than any other animals.

Open wide

Crocodilians lying with their mouths open on the river bank are exposing the inside of their mouth. The thin skin inside the mouth is well-supplied with blood, to absorb more heat from the sun.

Habitat and climate

Crocodilians can live wherever the climate is warm enough, in the **tropical** and **subtropical** parts of the world, as long as there is enough water. Some crocodilians are able to live in places which have cold winters, such as northern India, Nepal, the south-eastern United States, and parts of China.

Even these crocodilians do not **hibernate**. Instead, they shelter from the coldest nights by sleeping at the bottom of rivers or lakes, where the water stays a little warmer. Their body processes slow down while they are asleep, and only their heart and brain are supplied with the normal amount of oxygen. When the oxygen in its lungs begins to run out, the sleeping crocodilian surfaces without waking up to take a breath of air.

Most crocodilians live in fresh water, but some species can tolerate salt water. The freshwater species are less widespread than those which are able to cross the sea. The two

Nile crocodiles can live anywhere in Africa, wherever there is water and enough to eat.

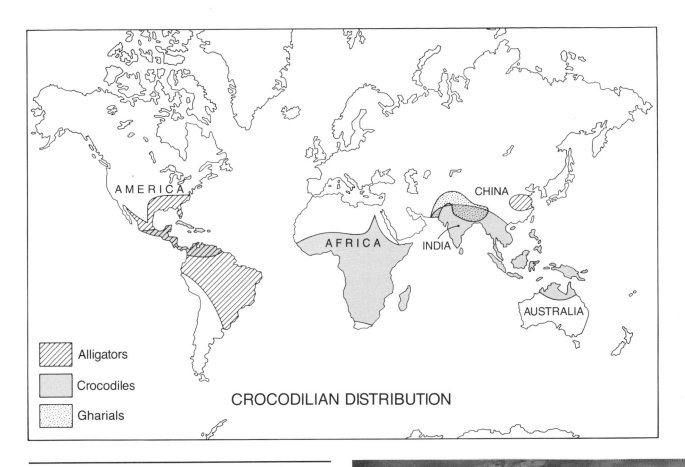

AMERICA

CHINA

AFRICA

INDIA

AUSTRALIA

Alligators

Crocodiles

Gharials

CROCODILIAN DISTRIBUTION

Right *The Mexican crocodile is one of the few crocodiles surviving in the Americas.*

most widespread species are both saltwater animals (see map above).

The most striking example of the advantage of being able to live on the sea shore is the Australian Saltwater crocodile. The 'salty' is found all over an enormous area, from India to Malaysia and northern Australia. Although it does not live in the open sea, over the ages it has been able to survive when washed across the ocean by storms, so that it has **colonized** new shores. In various countries in its range it has neighbours which can only live in fresh water, most of them in quite small areas. The freshwater crocodiles of New Guinea and northern Australia are two completely different species, even though they are separated only by a narrow strip of sea, dotted with islands. This is because salt water is a serious barrier to them and they die if they are washed out to sea.

7

Crocodilians of the world

There are 22 species of crocodilians in the world, divided into three families: the alligators, the true crocodiles and the gharial, which is different enough to have a family all to itself.

The main species of alligator are the American alligator (*Alligator mississippiensis*), which lives in the south-eastern United States; the black caiman (*Melanosuchus niger*) and the broad-snouted caiman (*Caiman latirostris*), which live in Central and South America; and the Chinese alligator (*Alligator sinensis*).

Crocodiles are much more widespread. The best-known is the Nile crocodile (*Crocodylus niloticus*), which lives in lakes and rivers all over tropical and southern Africa. Other African species include the dwarf crocodile (*Osteolaemus tetraspis*) and the slender-snouted crocodile (*Crocodylus cataphractus*). There are crocodiles in the Americas as well, including the American crocodile (*Crocodylus acutus*), the very rare Cuban crocodile (*Crocodylus rhombifer*), and the Orinoco crocodile (*Crocodylus intermedius*).

In India, the marsh crocodile or mugger (*Crocodylus palustris*) lives in rivers and swamps inland. In the Far East, the Siamese crocodile (*Crocodylus siamensis*), and the Philippine crocodile (*Crocodylus mindorensis*) live in rivers and estuaries, while the shores are dominated by the saltwater crocodile (*Crocodylus porosus*).

Left *A baby American alligator in Florida begins to hatch from its egg.*

Giants

Crocodiles are among the largest living reptiles. Although over-hunting has reduced the numbers of really large specimens, a few may still reach over 6 m in length. The longest recorded specimens of five species are: gharial 7.1 m; American crocodile 6.9 m; saltwater crocodile 6.8 m; American alligator 5.5 m; Indian mugger 4.0 m.

In northern Australia, the Australian fresh-water crocodile (*Crocodylus johnstoni*) lives mostly in pools and rivers away from the sea. Although it can live in salt or **brackish** water, it has never managed to cross the narrow channel to New Guinea, where the New Guinea crocodile (*Crocodylus novaeguinae*) has its home.

The gharial (*Gavialis gangeticus*) lives in rivers in north and eastern India, Pakistan, Bangladesh, and Nepal. It looks quite different from most other crocodilians, having a long, slender snout for catching fish. A species which lives in Malaysia, called the false gharial (*Tomistoma schlegelii*), looks rather like it, but is really a crocodile.

Most crocodilians are rare or endangered, as a result of being hunted for their skins.

Below *Gharials live in Nepal and India. These are in Chitwan National Park, Nepal.*

Bottom *The Siamese crocodile lives in fresh water, away from the coasts.*

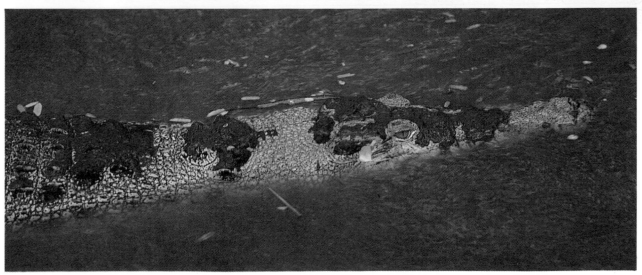

On the move

Because they are **aquatic** hunters, crocodilians are very good swimmers. In the water, they hold their legs folded back against their body. This gives them a **streamlined** shape, more like a fish. They swim with sweeping sideways movements of their tail, which is flattened from side to side, and has a ridge of scales to increase its area. The back feet are webbed, but they are not used in swimming; the webbing is an emergency escape mechanism. If a crocodilian sees danger approaching, it moves its hind feet sharply upwards with the toes spread out. This helps it to sink swiftly and silently below the surface.

Crocodilians are usually thought to be slow and clumsy on land. When they are not in a hurry or threatened, they crawl slowly on

American alligators crawl slowly along, until they feel threatened.

An Indian marsh crocodile, or mugger, can walk long distances over land.

their bellies in the same way as lizards, with their legs sprawling sideways and their elbows sticking up. The gharial and the saltwater crocodile have weak legs, and rarely crawl more than a metre or two from the water's edge. If danger suddenly appears, crocodilians *can* crawl quickly, slithering over the ground like a toboggan, down the bank and into the safety of the water.

All crocodilians can also walk with their legs nearly straight under their body, holding them clear of the ground. This 'high walk' enables some of them to move quite quickly on land, striding along rather like a mammal. The Indian marsh crocodile often wanders long distances away from water in this way.

Young crocodilians can use the front and back feet together to gallop, bounding along

Swallowing stones

Almost every adult crocodilian has stones in its stomach. These are found even when the animal lives in places like swamps, where stones are hard to find. The stones probably help to grind up its food, but they may also act as ballast when it swims.

like a squirrel. As they grow bigger they become too heavy to run in this way. The Australian freshwater crocodile is an exception – it can gallop across dry ground even when it is fully grown.

Hunting and feeding

Crocodilians are **carnivorous**. They are **scavengers** as well as **predators**. A crocodilian will eat any other animals that it can kill, including other crocodilians. As a crocodilian grows up, therefore, its range of **prey** changes to include larger animals.

Crocodilians with short broad snouts, like alligators and muggers, can kill everything from birds to medium-sized mammals. Alligators often catch herons by the legs, and they can crack open the shells of quite large turtles. Muggers have been known to kill large deer and even cattle. Like most crocodilians, a mugger lies in wait near the edge of water until an unsuspecting prey animal comes near enough to grab. Although there is no record of an elephant being hurt by a mugger, they will not go into water if they see a crocodile nearby.

The Nile crocodile feeds on a great variety of creatures during its life, from water bugs, snails and frogs when it is a baby, to fish and birds when it is a little older. Fully-grown Nile crocodiles still eat snails and fish, together with other reptiles, although they are also capable of killing and eating animals as big as a camel or a rhinoceros.

This Nile crocodile has caught an impala and dragged it under the water to drown.

American alligators have a varied diet. This one is eating a raccoon.

When it is eating an animal too large to be swallowed whole, a crocodile tears off chunks by seizing a piece in its jaws and spinning round in the water until the piece comes off.

The gharial, and a few other crocodiles which have the same long, slender snout, are fish-eaters. Their snouts are not especially strong, but they can be moved quickly through the water, to catch fish with a sideways sweep.

The fondness of crocodilians for **cannibalism** probably explains why young animals spend their early years among the vegetation in shallow water. They are hiding from their older relatives, who would eat them if they could find them.

Tooth-cleaning birds

Small shorebirds, especially the spur-winged plover, regularly use Nile crocodiles as a feeding place. They take leeches and blood-sucking flies from its skin. They also pick small particles of food from between the crocodile's teeth, even walking between the open jaws.

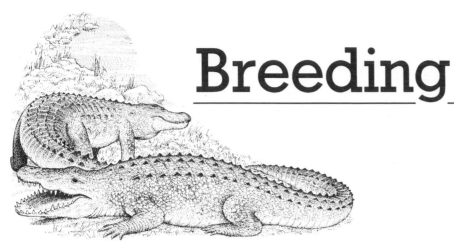

Breeding

During the breeding season, male crocodilians fight among themselves, often causing serious injuries and sometimes killing each other. These fights may be to defend a favourite basking place, or to drive another male away from a nearby female.

Male alligators and crocodiles both make sounds as part of their courtship, perhaps to attract females. Alligators roar loudly, vibrating their whole body. Other males hearing the roar join in, until the swamp echoes with their calls. Male Nile crocodiles make a coughing or barking noise, or a deep rumbling sound with their jaws wide open.

Once a male has attracted a female, he swims beside her until she lets him mate with her. She lays her eggs, which have hard shells

A baby saltwater crocodile lives on the yolk while it is inside the egg, like a bird.

Male crocodiles fight fiercely during the mating season. This one has lost a leg.

like those of birds, about two months after mating, choosing a place which is safe from flooding.

Female Nile crocodiles, and some other species, dig a hole in which to lay their eggs. The hole is usually in a shady place in sandy ground, and it may be as much as 60 cm deep, and more than 100 m from the water's edge. The female lays anything from 25 to 95 eggs, lowering them carefully into the hole with a back foot so that they do not crack. She then covers them over, and guards the place until the eggs hatch, ten or twelve weeks later. If she leaves for too long, the nest will be raided by monitor lizards or wild dogs, which like to eat the eggs.

When the young crocodiles hatch, they make a croaking sound. When the mother hears them, she loosens the sand – now baked hard by the sun – by wriggling on it. Mother Nile crocodiles escort or even carry their young from the nest site to the water.

The nesting of the American alligator, the Australian salty, and some caimans is so unusual that it needs a chapter to itself.

Gentle jaws

American alligators are regarded as primitive and fearsome creatures, and yet a female looks after her eggs and young in a very complicated and gentle way. It is now known that Australian saltwater crocodiles and some caimans make similar nests.

First, the female clears a patch of ground about 3 m across, by biting off and crushing the vegetation. She then makes a round pile of the broken plants, and hollows out the middle with her back feet. Into this hole she lays 15–80 eggs, covering them over with material from the edge of the nest, and with fresh

A female alligator defends her nest against any intruders . . .

. . . but she treats her small stripy babies very gently.

plants and mud which she fetches in her mouth. Finally, she crawls round and round the nest until it becomes a smooth cone, about 1 m high. The whole process is a lengthy one and may take as long as three or four nights.

The plant material sealed inside the mound begins to rot, like compost, warming up until it reaches a steady temperature of 30–32°C. This helps to incubate the eggs, while the mother keeps watch nearby, often lying on top of the nest to guard it.

While she is waiting for the eggs to hatch, the crocodilian also digs a pool nearby, away from the main body of water.

When the babies are ready to hatch, they stay underground, but stick their snouts out of their shells. When they feel the vibrations caused by their mother crawling nearby, they squeak. She digs them out of the nest, and carries them in her jaws to release them into the pool. She then picks up any eggs which have not hatched, and gently cracks them in her jaws until each baby can escape.

Some female alligators in the Florida Everglades have been observed looking after their babies for as long as two years.

These baby alligators are being raised on an alligator farm.

Dundee's crocodiles

Kakadu National Park, in northern Australia, became famous when part of the film *Crocodile Dundee* was made there. The park is also the home of the largest remaining populations of two species of Australian crocodiles: the salt-water crocodile, or 'salty', and its freshwater cousin.

The salty dominates the estuaries and the seashores. Its ferocity is infamous; there are many stories of people being killed. Fishermen have been dragged from their boats, and swimmers have been attacked, not only in the water, but while they stood on the bank. The crocodiles approach underwater, leaping up the bank at the last moment and grabbing at the person's legs. They are said to be the only wild animals which actually hunt people as prey.

The main reason for contacts between crocodiles and people in northern Australia *was* hunting, but by the people, not the crocodiles. The skin of the crocodile's belly is valuable because it makes fine leather for clothes, shoes and handbags. As a result salties were almost wiped out, except in the most remote corners of Northern Territory. Nowadays many salties are drowned in fishing nets.

Scientists who studied the salties to find a way of protecting them also collected information about the freshwater crocodile. They found that in places where the salty had been wiped out, the so-called freshwater crocodile

The dreaded saltwater crocodile, or 'salty', on a beach in northern Australia.

Good advice for visitors to Florida. American alligators can be as dangerous as salties.

was to be found in brackish estuaries, close to the sea, and not solely in lakes and rivers inland. It can in fact tolerate some salt in the water. However, it had been restricted to inland waters in the past by competition with the much bigger, and fiercer, saltwater species.

Nevertheless, it is unable to live in full seawater, which is why it has never come into contact with its close neighbour, the New Guinea freshwater crocodile.

Storing food in larders

Crocodilians are often said to hide freshly-killed food, perhaps to let it rot until it is tender enough to eat. Although there are several hunters' tales reporting this habit, it has never been confirmed by a **naturalist**.

The fish-eaters

All crocodilians eat a lot of fish, but some, among them the Australian and New Guinea freshwater crocodiles, eat little else. Their main adaptation for fishing is the narrow snout. Other fish specialists are the African slender-snouted crocodile, and the gharials, true and false. Fish-eating crocodilians have particularly sharp teeth, to pierce and hold their slippery prey. All crocodilians have a **valve** in their throat which closes the windpipe when they open their mouth underwater.

Some fish-eaters chase their prey, but the more usual way of catching it is to lie in ambush and wait for it to swim near, grabbing it with a sudden sideways sweep of the jaws.

Below *The gharial's slender snout can be moved quickly through the water to catch fish.*

Above *Alligators are not specialists, but they catch and eat a lot of fish.*

Opposite top *In Venezuela, caimans are important in the food chain. This one has caught a large electric eel.*

Large fish may be dragged ashore, and sometimes killed by being beaten on a rock.

The broad-snouted caiman also feeds mainly on fish. When most of the caimans in the central Amazon basin were killed by hunters, they expected the fishing to improve, but the reverse happened. The reason was the complicated **food chain**. The lakes where the fish **fry** grow up are very poor in the **nutrients** which enable plants to grow. Since the fish fry feed on plants, and on small plant-eating animals, the whole fish population depends on the plants being provided with nutrients from outside the lake. The hunters discovered too late that the essential link in the food chain was the caimans.

This is how it worked. The little fish were eaten by larger fish, as well as birds, otters, turtles – and caimans. The caimans, at the top of the food chain, would eat all the other predators as well, when they could catch them. It turned out that the main source of nutrients for the plants in the lakes was the droppings of visiting caimans. When the caimans were wiped out, the plants failed to grow, the fish fry had nothing to feed on, and the whole food chain collapsed.

Fish sanctuaries

Alligator holes, made by mothers to protect their young, are important for the fish and birds of the Florida Everglades. At times, when the water is low, the holes are the only place where fish can survive. Fish-eating birds then come to gather food for their young from the packed pools.

Fear and fascination

Everybody seems to be afraid of crocodiles and alligators. Even people in Europe, who have never seen one in the wild, know the stories brought back by early explorers from Africa, Asia and the Americas. The fear is much older than that. The ancient Egyptians worshipped crocodiles, and some of their beliefs passed on to the Greeks and Romans. There are many ancient **legends** about them in the Far East, even in Japan, where there are no crocodilians. Most of the stories arise from a natural fascination with the size and strength of the animals.

The best known are the tales of dragons and maidens, and the brave knights who rode

The fearsome jaws and spiny back of a crocodile gave rise to stories of dragons.

A mugger in Sri Lanka. It is believed that crocodiles were once fed human sacrifices.

to their rescue. Some of these stories may have been true. Crocodiles lived in the marshes near Haifa, in Israel, until the early years of this century, and in ancient times they may have been fed human sacrifices.

St George of England is supposed to have killed a dragon to save a maiden. He lived long after the sacrifices stopped, but it is quite possible that one of these old tales was added on to his life story by Crusaders who heard it in the Holy Land. There are several churches in France where stuffed Nile crocodiles used to be on show, labelled as the remains of dragons.

There were many tales of crocodiles eating people in Africa, Asia, Burma and Sri Lanka. Many horror stories were brought home to terrify Europeans; and when Europeans began to settle in the countries from which the stories came, the crocodilians there were in great danger.

Dangerous to humans?

Only two species, the Nile crocodile and the saltwater crocodile, regularly attack humans. They both have a very wide range, and everywhere they live the local people keep out of their way. Reports of other species eating people are rare, and probably exaggerated. Although the gharial can grow to be the biggest of all crocodilians, people who live by lakes and rivers in India are not afraid of it. They show more respect for the mugger, though it very rarely attacks people.

However, when European settlers arrived in places where crocodilians were common, they were afraid. When the Seychelles (islands of the coast of East Africa) were first colonized in 1770, there were huge saltwater crocodiles living in the mangrove swamps round the coast. The settlers killed them all in the first few years. There is still a place called Crocodile Bay, but there are no crocodiles.

Towards the end of World War II, nearly a thousand Japanese soldiers were killed by hundreds of saltwater crocodiles, as they tried to wade across a swamp at night. Such mass attacks are very rare, though a few individual swimmers are attacked each year in northern

People in India are wary of the mugger, although it rarely attacks humans.

Australia, in the places where salties are still common. More often, the victims are hunters who were trying to kill the crocodiles.

Elsewhere, even though the crocodilians are not dangerous, people are afraid of them, probably because of the stories they have heard. In Florida, where large areas of marshy land have been drained to build houses, alligators live in ornamental pools on the estates. Cats and dogs often disappear without trace, but there have been very few authenticated attacks on humans. But people still shoot alligators, or call on the government to get rid of them. It would be more to the point to ask whether people are dangerous to crocodilians.

Recipes for indigestion

A Nile crocodile which was shot in South Africa was found to contain the identity discs from 22 dogs. In the same way muggers on the Ganges are often found to contain human remains, which they have scavenged after funerals. Nile crocodiles are sometimes found with bottles in their stomachs: they probably picked them up instead of stones.

A mugger is quite likely to grab an unwary bird, such as this white heron.

Dangerous to crocodilians?

Wherever people live, crocodilians are in danger because of hunting. Before firearms were common, it was a more equal contest; against people armed only with ropes and spears, the crocodilian would quite often win the fight. Similar methods are still used in some remote parts of Malaysia and Borneo, but the main reason for them is the **ritual** killing of crocodilians that eat people, not to get food or leather.

Once guns became common, crocodilians were in great danger. There are many examples from all over the world of the sort of thing that happened to the salties in the Seychelles. At the mouth of the River Amazon, between 1900 and 1910, as many as 400 caimans were killed every day by sports hunters who shot them from passing boats. Because of this campaign of **extermination**, caimans soon became rare in the area.

Crocodilians are also killed accidentally when they are trapped and drowned in fishing nets. This is why the American crocodile is so rare among the Keys, the islands south of Florida, off the coast of North America. But the main threat to crocodilians from people is **commercial** hunting.

At one time, crocodile skin was very valuable because it was fashionable for shoes and handbags, so the hunters were out in force. Crocodilians are very easy to shoot as they lie quietly in the water, and large numbers were

Opposite below *Until fairly recently Nile crocodiles were hunted for their skins, but also for sport.*

Above *The American alligator depends on human control of its water level. On the bank is a terrapin.*

killed in a short time. Most species became rare after very few years of hunting.

In Florida, for example, 190 000 alligators were killed in 1929. By 1934, although the price had doubled, the hunters could only catch 120 000. In 1943, when the price was over ten times what it was in 1929, the hunters could kill only 6800 alligators.

The same has happened in New Guinea and northern Australia to the saltwater crocodile, in Africa to the Nile crocodile, and to the gharial and the mugger in India.

Nests drowned by people

Water enters the Everglades from farm-lands to the north. The rate is controlled by a computer, which is supposed to imitate natural rainfall cycles. However, during heavy rains, large amounts of water are released, and many alligator nests are flooded and the eggs drowned.

Protecting crocodilians

Since 1944, after they were nearly wiped out by commercial hunting, alligators have been protected in the United States. The protection has worked. Although they have lost a great deal of their **habitat** to farmland and housing estates, the population has recovered, and American alligators are no longer in so much danger of extinction.

The gharial in India and Nepal also became rare because of hunting. In 1974, there may have been less than 100 left alive. The Indian government set up sanctuaries, where gharial eggs, collected from the wild, could be

This baby gharial is hatching in a sanctuary, where it will be safe.

Opposite above *American crocodiles. The last few are carefully protected.*

Opposite below *Crocodiles remind us of a time before humans ruled in the world.*

hatched in safety. The babies are released when they are over 1.2 m long, and safe from predators. There are now several thousand gharials, in the sanctuaries and in the wild, and though the species is still not really safe, its future looks more promising.

The same cannot be said for the saltwater crocodiles in Australia. Although they are protected from commercial hunting, they are still feared by people. In many towns and villages in Queensland, for example, they can legally be killed on sight. They are safe in the national parks, but that is only a small part of their former range.

In Africa, North and South America, and even in Israel, crocodilians are now raised on farms, like cattle, to be killed for meat and skins. This protects the wild populations from hunting, though there is still some **poaching**.

In southern India, the Madras Crocodile Bank is a breeding centre from which crocodilians can be released into safe places in the wild. It is also open to the public, so that people can come and look at the animals, perhaps to learn to respect these magnificent reptiles rather than to fear them.

Like lions and tigers, grizzly bears and elephants, crocodilians have a right to survive. They are a reminder of the time before humans took over the world.

GLOSSARY

Aquatic Living or growing in or on water.

Bask To lie in the sun to get warm.

Brackish Slightly salty.

Cannibalism The eating of members of one's own species.

Carnivorous Meat-eating.

Cold-blooded Having a body temperature that varies with that of the surrounding air.

Colonized Settled in or occupied.

Commercial An activity undertaken for profit.

Extermination To get rid of by destroying completely.

Food chain The natural sequence in which small animals eat plants, and then are eaten by larger animals.

Fossil The remains of a long-dead animal which have become part of a rock.

Fry The young of a fish.

Habitat The environment in which an animal usually lives.

Hibernate To sleep through the winter.

Legend An old story which may not be true.

Naturalist A person who studies natural history.

Nutrient Food; the chemicals a plant or animal needs in order to grow.

Poaching Illegally killing protected animals.

Predator An animal that lives by preying on other animals.

Prey An animal which is eaten by another.

Ritual A religious or solemn ceremony.

Scavenger An animal which eats the remains of dead animals.

Streamlined Smooth in shape, in order to pass through the water easily in the case of crocodilians.

Subtropical The regions of the earth, next to the tropical regions, that have no cold season.

Tropical The warmer regions of the earth near the equator.

Valve A structure which controls the movement of fluids in a pipe, in this case a crocodilian's windpipe.

Index

The entries in **bold** are illustrations.

Picture Acknowledgements

The publishers would like to thank the
Survival Anglia picture library, London, England,
and the following photographers for the use
of photographs on the pages listed:

Maurice Tibbles 4, 6, 26; Mike Price 5, 9 (top), 20 (top and bottom), 28; John Harris 7; Jeff Simon 8, 16 (top); Dieter and Mary Plage 9 (bottom), 11, 23; Jeff Foott 10, 13, 15, 16 (bottom), 17, 19, 21, 22, 27, 29, 30; Alan Root 12; Michael Kavanagh 24; Johanna Van Gruisen 25.

The publishers would like to thank Oxford Scientific Films for the use of photographs on pages 14 and 18.

About the author

Malcolm Penny has a B.Sc. Hons degree in zoology from Bristol University in England and led the Bristol Seychelles Expedition in 1964. He was also a member of the Royal Society Expedition to the Aldabra Islands off the coast of Tanzania in 1966. Malcolm has worked for the Wildfowl Trust and was the First Scientific Administrator for the International Council for Bird Preservation on Cousin Island in the Seychelles. He now works as a producer of natural history programs for Survival Anglia, the internationally renowned wildlife film-makers based in Norwich, England.